Farm to Table

Keep On Truckin'

Volume III – Faith Walker

ROCK

Farm To Table

Keep On Truckin'

Volume III – Faith Walker

Copyright © 2021

by ROCK

Printed in the United States of America by Kindle Direct Publishing

Some names and identifying details have been changed to protect the privacy of individuals. Readers should be aware that Internet Web sites offered as citations and/or sources for further information may have changed or disappeared between the time this was written and when it is read.

ISBN: 9798403861182

Foreword

I can remember being around semi's since I was a kid. My daddy, stepdad, and a couple of boyfriends were truckers. My first love was a trucker. I even had driven a semi across Arizona, but ended up in management in convenience stores. I met Roxanne (aka Rock), about 20 years ago. We met at a church in Jefferson, GA. I was in a difficult time in my life. Now I see the Lord brought her to help me. I remember thinking that this woman was different than anyone I have been around. She and I were as different as day and night, but in some ways had experienced some of the same trials in life.

She has and is still helping me through this unpredictable life. We are special friends with good days and bad days.

Like the difference between my Southern Phrases and her Vegas Lingo with "jabs" LOL!

She has told me countless times, the Holy Spirit told her we would work together, and we have, whether it be at jobs or ministries, including being friends. Roxanne (Rock) has always walked in Faith with the Lord. When you read this book and the other ones, you will see just how much Faith will get you through life by her own experiences.

I am writing this foreword with honor and respect for all the experiences she has dealt with in her life, and she still walks in Faith daily.

Bobbie Finch Weaver
Aka Bob Weav
Special Friend for Life

1

Creating a Path
in the Forest

 As you recall in Volume II of The Farm to Table Series, "Risky Business", I told you that I got thrown out of the small town of Hoschton, Georgia. We left a 2-bedroom 1-bath ranch house we called "the Panther Creek home" to go to a piece of land with 8-acres out in the bush of Jackson County, Georgia. Semis, or as some call them, "transfer trucks", are so big, so in a small town, they look even bigger. So did the hundred-year-old oak trees.

There were so many trees that needed to be taken down for us to even drive down the driveway.

I had a lot of house plans, hopes, and dreams that Jed and a bunch of the young kids didn't have, but we had a plan to call this home in the trees, ours. So, I didn't really blame the kids or Jed for that matter – I didn't know how, I just knew that we could do it. Why? Because I found out in my journey that I am a true "Faith Walker".

So, I stick my faith out there. (That's a scripture, I found out later) – and tell Jed and all six kids to load up in the truck (it was an old Ford truck with wooden bed rails Jed had made). I said, "We're going out to the property to see where we're going to build our new home."

ROCK

We all jumped in the truck and I got my smokes figuring I'd need a crutch of some sort to even think of how this is going to happen… and off we go. The kids were loaded up in the back of the truck, Jed was driving, and I was sitting shotgun to head to the property to look at the dirt we'd soon call "The Ponderosa!"

As we come over the overpass of 85, we start slowing down to see a break in the trees where our new land was. The kids were excited, but unsure, and like anything new, they wanted to check it out. So then we find a break in the trees where the lady with the Caddy first took me down to look at the land.

The trees were whipping the kids in the face and the anticipation of what they were about to see was definitely happening. They were giggling, laughing, and yelling, "Hey mom, is this it?"

I basically yelled back, "Yes, shut it! We'll be there in a few minutes after we dodge these trees." We pull up, Jed put it in park, and the kids jumped out. What they saw first blew them away! It was just a slab of concrete in a clearing with a single toilet on it and a half-built wall where it looked like they started the concrete but stopped and gave up.

I recall the kids ages 4-14 were saying, "Really Mom? We're supposed to sleep where? What are we supposed to do?" All the typical questions kids would ask. They didn't have a clue what kind of work would be in store for them. They didn't have the vision for the whole family that I did.

They had no clue and neither did I. I mean, I kind of did, but Jed was looking at it like, "How are we going to do anything?" I knew right then and there it was going to take a whole lot of work, love, devotion and faith to change this concrete slab into a home.

I had been so overwhelmed with the crap I had already been through, that I just smiled because I finally got to GA. I thought, "Okay, this is going to be very hard, but it's very beautiful out here and those awesome oak trees" So much quietness and beauty.

I knew I had found one of the priceless pieces of Heaven on Earth and all I had to do was stay consistent with the good guy voice and "Keep on Truckin'". I don't think I'll ever forget what those kids looked like in the back of that Ford truck.

The anticipation of what they would see was much like me when I saw the Cadillac lady. I had to have the optimistic side for the kids and Jed.

Me, Jed, and the kids were always saying, "We got this", not even knowing what we were saying. Ha-ha!

But I would definitely find out. I knew one thing: first things first – we need to create a real path throughout the forest to the top of the hill where there was one slab and a toilet. We needed to create a path through the forest, we have to make a path. What does that mean?

What that meant to me was: My checkbook had a dollar, and I had a pack of kids that were being sent from Ohio to Georgia due to the divorce-spirit running rampant. Everybody must play their part for the kids.

So, as you're reading this, just know that it's a nightmare to deal with, but I knew that the kids would be better off for it. They would be the next leaders on the planet. I was bound and determined to do my part in raising them. Things that shouldn't be in the way had to be removed, so that they would learn how to build strong families and relationships. Even if they were laughing in my face, there's an old saying – "Those who laugh last laugh best". This is my cue, let's do this.

2

Digging In

Being a trucker, you know that everything we have got here on a truck, one way or another. So, my first problem to solve was how was I going to get a machine to dig into this piece of heaven? One

thing I know now that I didn't know then, was that if you're smack dab in the middle of God's Will, He provides everything you need.

Everybody always thinks it's about money and the big majority of people live this way, but the truth is, it's all about FAITH. What is faith? Faith is the substance of things HOPED FOR, and the evidence of things not seen. So, there you have it. I hoped for the machines and all the rest, and suddenly by God's grace, some dude that does clearing showed up in my little office in the square of Hoschton.

He needed help with trucking, and I needed him and his machine to clear the land so we could at least access the land and clear it and start building something. So, being a wheeler and dealer from Las Vegas, I made a deal with this dude, trading my skills in trucking for his skills in land clearing.

I sent Jed out to the property to meet the clearing guy. I had threatened Jed's life (not really), more like just warned him, because I didn't want my hundred-year-old oak trees to be taken out by a bunch of men who just wanted to hurry up and clear something.

ROCK

So, Jed acted like he had it under control until I got nudged by a voice to go out there and check it out. I got out there and by the Grace of God, I stood in front of that machine, it was a big, giant bulldozer.

I stood before the old dude that was running it and stopped him from taking out more trees. He was having a field day, but I knew this property would be beautiful if it was done correctly, as long as they only took out trees that were necessary.

I had a blueprint of a beautiful lane with a fence; there was a beautiful pasture on both sides where the home would be built. You could stand on the deck and see an awesome lawn pegged with Glory. WOW. This was how I was going to do this, and with my dude on the machine, I was right on time to keep him from taking all the out or it would have been a whole different story, I just knew it. I told the old dude on the dozer, "Stop your madness, no more trees. You're done. Stop!"

Jed was trying to find me so he could take out more trees, talking about the semis and how they needed room to move, and I got that – but I let him know right quick he best draw it and show me before he went after another tree. I found out later, "Write the Vision, Make it Plain, so he who sees it can run with it."

Well, there you go. I always wondered why I enjoyed my "things-to-do" list, because most of the time if you write it on paper, you'll do it and you'll see it come to pass. And so, I saw it on paper first cause I'm a "things-to-do" list guy. And that's why architects are so needed, because they draw your vision.

ROCK

So, a little advice to my readers: if you wanna do something easy, or have anything worth doing, write it down. So, back to the story; one thing I know is I needed manpower to help me and I had enough wood to stay warm for a very long time. I found out later I could have sold those trees for a pretty penny.

But no, I was bound and determined to do it my way – which between you and me, I didn't even really know what that meant. It basically just meant, like anything else I ever tried to conquer, I wanted to do it my way.

One step at a time. I learned later that there was a scripture that reads "I can do all things through Christ who strengthens me". I personally thought I had the power to do all things, but truth be told, God was helping me do everything. So, the road was finally in, and we bought a small two-man camper that was ugly, but it would become my home for two years at the top of the hill, by the slab of concrete, on the property, everything that had to be done was directed from the top of that hill.

It was living in the mountains, it cold. It was in the snow, rain, wind, and all the things you don't consider when building something you have a vision for. It was very hard. If I hadn't been trained as a kid in Las Vegas to just deal with the circumstances, I know there's no way I could have done it alone.

My faith was being tested to the greatest degree. First things first, I found a carpenter named Cooper, (most called him "Coop"). He was 70 years old when he took on this project of building my home in the middle of nowhere. Back then, old man Coop had a serious southern drawl. He'd say, "Roxanne, I believe I can do this fer ya, do you got some plans?" BOY DID I!

ROCK

Remember in the second Volume, "Risky Business", I went to the closing and the chick sold me the plans for $35. Well, I found out it was Coop who needed them. He hired a bunch of men for $5/hr., which back then was a deal to have a real home builder to build, but I didn't have the first clue what to do.

Coop said, "Well Roxanne, the first thing you got to do is have some wood." YAY – I was in the lumber business. Trucking, wood, and building materials; that's what I did with my trucks. So, I had to ask Coop how much wood he needed. "Well Roxanne, (in his southern drawl, while smoking his Camel non filters) "You better get me a truckload".

So, here I go trying to figure out how I'm going to get the old man Coop a load of wood. Just like anything you ever hope for or need, I just started talking about it to anyone who would listen, from my customers who I hauled for, to the men at the little restaurant in town where I ate breakfast in the mornings.

Then I get a call one day from a man I did hauling for in Virginia. He owned a sawmill and heard about my little dilemma through the grapevine (back then, it was a serious trucking grapevine). He asked if he gave me the lumber, would I do some hauling for him and move some material at the saw-mill – and we traded out like the old barter system: "you do this, I'll do that."

I said, "Okay, I'll get my truck up there to you in Virginia. I think his name was Joe…. we made it happen. I wanna say his name was Joe, I don't know, but what I do know is that he had the wood, and he was in Virginia.

So I sent my truck, (that looks like the one on the cover, a white cab over Pete) with my driver Randy, to Virginia. Next thing I know, Coop has the wood at the property – the next problem to solve was carpenters.

So, I told the old man, "Okay, let's make it happen and start building this thing." Most people that were around me thought I had a million dollars stashed somewhere and they had more faith in me than I did in myself, which was good

They expected me to produce, so I did. I went to the People's Bank in Winder, GA to get a building loan and they laughed in my face. I went to every loan establishment you could think of. Would anybody help a poor struggling one-man-show trucker? NO! NO! NO! It was always the answer. That's when I met Phil.

Phil was a pawn broker. Now, I really went through it with Phil. He believed in me, but couldn't stand Jed, and for good reason. He was always complaining about the things I wasn't doing right instead of the great things that were happening. It pissed Phil off. He would end up playing a key role for me in my building, that is now called "The Ponderosa".

Remember, all of us need someone to believe in our dreams and visions and back us up. I really didn't know at the time, but now I know it. Now Phil was a very large man, who looked just like Herman Munster from the Munster's back in the day. He would always tell me it was always about money, and I'd tell him it wasn't (though, that was the reason he helped me with money for the project).

I'd go on and on about God and how He helped me and saved me so many times.

ROCK

Phil was like "yeah yeah yeah, how much do you need?" He was kind and would always help me to pay my men. He even waited 'til I got paid to take care of him.

(He would hold checks, for a large fee so it helped me and him).

"The Ponderosa" started to take form. Jed was basically pissed most of the time because, well, honestly, I think he was just pissed that we had to work so hard, and he didn't want to. He just wanted to go to that dumb racetrack or play his guitar and bump working.

Well, when you take on the kind of climate I did to build a working ranch atmosphere that was conducive to truckers, It's a lot of work. I like to work, he really didn't, but praise God I found a bunch of men that wanted to.

Most of the time, around 4 o'clock, all the men would start drinking beer, including Jed. Coop didn't drink so he'd leave the job around 3:30. He was a good ol' boy from way back and he knew how to lead a team.

Coop was extremely disciplined. Every morning he was on the job at 8:00am and left every day at 3:30pm. He smoked camel non filters and squatted a lot while he would think about the jobs. He was a kind man, tall, slender and you knew he was raised right. He grew up farming back in the day and he understood an honest days work.

Coop brought a lot of joy to me since he wasn't pushy, and he had a very patient soul! He laughed a lot and told good, clean jokes to the men.

ROCK

He had a lot of respect for me being so young and choosing to build the hard way, so he took real good care of me in making sure I was happy with his job, right on down to my cabinets.

He was a cabinet maker too. He designed my cabinets to last forever and made sure there were plenty of them. I loved him for being there for me and always having my back on the building project with the men. He was an old warhorse and the men really respected him.

He was a true blessing sent to me; I believe to keep me calm in the storm of the building project. He'd always say in his southern drawl "Don't worry about this Roxanne, we got this!" Somehow, I believed he could do anything!

3
Raising the Walls

So here goes Coop, leading the pack. Got the carpenters out there making it happen. It started finally looking like something. I was really happy that it looked like like it did, but when the newness and reality set in, it was on with Jed. His drinking started becoming a nightmare. I was stuck in a two-man camper with a little TV, fridge, and a typewriter in the window, where I did the billing for my customers. I had nowhere to run, all my kids were in Florida and Ohio until we at least got the home framed in.

So, I was alone out in the dark, in a camper, in the middle of nowhere with a drunk dude. Jed didn't talk a lot at first, but when he would get on a roll, it was "blah blah blah", calling me names like "bitch, whore, slut" all the time.

He had a friend named Paulie who played the lead guitar and was extremely good. He actually won the trophy for "Best Lead Guitar" in Georgia. He was a very nice man. He'd listen to me tell him what was going on with Jed and he'd say, "Rock, love doesn't call you a bitch, whore or slut." This is before I learned that God is love.

I just figured that because I gave my word, and promised to live until death do us part, that this was part of it, and I was just supposed to deal with it. I'm pretty sure there are a lot of people who have done or are even doing the same thing now. Hear me now, it's bad – it's wrong – RUN FOR YOUR LIFE!!

ROCK

Okay back to the story. Winter set in at "The Ponderosa" and it was freezing. The walls were up, but there was plastic on the walls, windows, and doors. There was a plank to walk over to get in the house. You had to cross a mote to get in the house. The kids were begging to come stay with me even though the house was in this state, so we brought Sammy from Florida and Dana from Ohio.

They wanted to go to school and live with us, but I told them how brutal it would be – they didn't care. I got them some mattresses for the basement concrete slab and a torpedo heater (the men used it on outside jobs). They also had a makeshift toilet and water that the construction dudes had used. They dealt with it. They were about 14 years old and would carry kerosene down to the basement for their own heaters to keep from freezing.

It helped me a lot to see them tough it out, and it showed me what it's like to have a home come together little by little.

They felt sorry for me having to live with Jed and his mouth. They would come to the camper and say, "Mom are you okay?" I'd lie and tell them I was great, but they saw right through it. Dana saw through his dad too and called him out one night when he was drunk on Yukon Jack. We knew this was a demon.

Dana bowed up on him and said, "I know who you are, and I'm not scared of you, come on!" Jed pulled a gun out. There were some people there too: Two men, Jody, and Kyle (who were just there to visit.) We made it a practice to never call the law on someone unless it was truly out of control. In this case, it looked pretty bad enough to call.

ROCK

It was the same old drill.

I went in and dialed 911. It seemed they were working it out when I walked back outside. I had told Jody to go to the top of the hill to stop the cops. Well, she tried, but they ended up asking who lived there. She told them his name and they bolted right down the lane. He was so known, they had nicknamed him. "The Colonel". Kyle was so scared. He was only four years old.

I wasn't scared of any of them, I just didn't want my kids to be involved or see this kind of whacking. I'd seen it myself since I lived it in Vegas.

So, the cops disarmed Jed, talked it out, and said it was just a punk kid coming out at his dad and they left. But Dana was right, it was a demon, and it really did want to kill him – it just didn't want to go to jail.

Okay let's get back to the building project. We had a well that was dug, and boy, was it a project! We had some of the best water on the planet though. We were "sitting on a stream", the dude said. What a blessing! I knew it was time to bring the water to the house.

Remember my secretary back at Ken Rock Trucking BC? Well, she dug up some gravediggers to dig my water line to the house. She said all they wanted was a case of Old Milwaukee.

Well, that was a deal! I couldn't believe it. These dudes dug by hand the fastest water line I'd ever seen. I gave them their penance, their Old Milwaukee, and on their way they went. Now we had running water to the house, a very big deal for us! No windows, no doors, no heat or air, but water – yes. It was exciting

4

Water

People don't really get it. Water is everything! You can't do anything without it. When I see the kids on TV drinking that filthy water, I have such a heart for it because I know what it's like to not have water on tap. We take it for granted that we can just turn on a spigot and out comes hot and cold water, not me man! I will, TO THIS DAY, take out anyone who wastes water. I turn into a weirdo and start yelling "DON'T WASTE THAT WATER!

It's funny how God will use the things that you went through that bother you most to bless someone else with what ticks you off, but He does. Just a simple bath was a big deal. Coop found me a makeshift bathtub with a shower for $75.00 and with his southern drawl said, "Roxanne, ya want me to put this in fer ya so you can take a bath?" I was ecstatic, "YES I DO!" I won't ever forget.

That was an amazing bathtub experience, sitting in my bathtub with no walls, but it was mine and I could soak – it was wonderful. No more showers at the Truck-stop, which was getting pretty old.

"Quick, hurry up – take a shower and get dressed" was OVER and I could actually just chill. It was AMAZING GRACE.

ROCK

The moral of this part of the story is basically: Don't take for granted the simple things we have, like running water, or even hot water on tap. I was very blessed and thankful to have water, to say the least.

Water changed our lives! Somehow, we didn't mind walking the plank to get into the kitchen that was studded out. We got a sink and stove from somewhere and even without walls, we could cook and maybe dig out some dishes. We really don't realize how blessed we are to have water. We couldn't even exist without it.

I learned not to take that simple thing for granted, and to be thankful for every drop. Somehow, I didn't think people really got it. Water is a precious commodity, and we should all be thankful for it.

God knows me and the kids were so thankful, it changed everything for us out there.

Just like little Kyle, as he was getting older around six or seven, his dad Russ said he could go live with his mommy when she got some walls. So, Kyle would call me and say "Mommy, do you have any walls yet?" But, bless his heart, the answer at that time was still "No". But things were looking better in trucking.

Jed wanted two more trucks, so I told him, "Okay, go find some." He did. He found a guy in Gainesville, which I later found out was nicknamed "GainesVegas". I laughed because I made a Vegas deal with a guy in Gainesville, Georgia for Jed's second truck. It was red, which is on the first book.

ROCK

I used it until I could get far enough into this story to picture all of this. But I've been told by some other friends to put some pictures in my volumes for you. As I'm telling the story, I see the pictures you should see.

One day, I was at the office in Hoschton working and one of the kids came home from school and called me and said, "Way to go Mom". They said, "Way to get us some insulation for the house." I said, "Why do you say that? Is someone there?" They said, "Yes, they are on stilts walking around the kitchen putting in, guess what, insulation!" I didn't order it, so I laughed and said I'd be right home.

I get there and there are two dudes almost finished with the kitchen, and the dining area and a whole bunch of rooms with insulation. **31**

I said, "Guys, who's your boss?" They gave me his number. I called him and said, "Sir, you have a couple of your men at my house finishing the insulation, but you know, and I know that I've never talked to you in my life."

He said, "Wow really?" He was mad and I was a little ruthless back then and said, "I don't want to get you for trespassing." "My bad," he said. "Keep the insulation and get my guys out of there." It was a true miracle. We didn't have money for insulation.

Don't think God won't provide all your needs. It wasn't a want, it was a need. Winter was setting in, we're in the North Georgia Mountains. It gets cold. We only had plastic on the windows and doors, so it was quite a blessing. Even though we had water, I'd still send the kids to the laundromat to do the fifteen loads of laundry.

ROCK

They'd sit on the washer and dryers every Saturday and take all day and every machine to wash the clothes. They were learning what it was like to build something from the ground up and how to work together as a team to make it happen.

To this day, they appreciate the so-called "torture" it was to live in that kind of environment, building by faith.

One random day, I was just walking around looking at what needed to happen next... I knew we needed heat. All I did was mention this to a guy I knew and there was a heater dude knocking on the camper door. I brought him to the house and showed him what was going on. He couldn't believe it. He said, "You know, I'm impressed that you'd even try to build this house like this. I'll help you with heating and air." I was pretty jacked up about that, I didn't have the money for it, but he said I could pay him little by little until it was paid for.

Wow! I knew God was working this out for me. He said he'd send a crew out and get it put in for me. I knew it was a God thing. That changed everything. The heat was really needed. We were freezing just trying to walk around the half-built place.

5

Faith Prevails

It was freezing by now in the Georgia mountains. I had a temporary power pole that was pulling the heating and air and my power bill went skyrocketing to $1500. Because it was so high, the power company came out to see what was going on. The dude couldn't believe it.

He said, "Lady you can't have a temporary power pole and run a heating and air unity with no walls to stay warm." I said, "What should I do?" The guy went on to say he'd never seen anything like it and said he'd get back to me around November.

It gets super cold in November. The kids were still using their torpedo heater in the basement, and it smelled like kerosene all the time.

I decided to build a makeshift office in one of the rooms, like a bigger base station than the camper. I was running the heat wide open and just knew if I had some windows and doors I could contain the heat, so I was on a mission.

Jed was watching TV one night and saw a commercial for windows and gave me the number. I called the company and got one of their salesmen to come out and give me a quote on the windows for the giant house. Well, the dude arrived and was blown away. He said, "Why didn't you put the windows in before you put the siding on?"

I said, "I've never built a house before, I don't know the stages." He thought I was a weirdo. So, he gave me a quick quote with some gigantic amount like fifteen-grand and then tried to leave. I said, "Hey dude, I need some windows".

He said, "Cough up fifteen grand and I'll give you some". I told him I didn't have any money, but I still needed windows. Well, this dude was shocked because he couldn't believe I was still pushing him for the windows with no money, but I had a whole lot of faith. But remember: Faith is the substance of things hoped for and the evidence of things not seen.

He said, "I feel sorry for you lady, but I've got to leave. Hope you can find someone to help you." I told him he needed to help me, and my motto was "if there's a will, there's a way." He said, "There's nothing I can do, hope you make it, bye." He took off on the path of the red mud and he thought he had escaped helping me.

Well, the dude with the windows could run, but he couldn't hide. I had the income of two trucks running on the road, a half-built house, and winter was setting in. I called the window guy every day for a couple of weeks. He was ditching my calls until one day he said, "Lady, what do you want? I told you I couldn't help you."

I said there's always a way. I need you. I need you to figure out how to do this. He said, "Why are you torturing me with this? Call someone else." I told him I was prompted to hammer him about the windows. He asked by who? I told him, "I think it's God." Now he was really freaked out. He told me to lose his number.

So, I waited for a couple of weeks, and didn't call him – and one day out of the blue he called me. He said, "Look lady, I can't sleep or get you out of my mind. You told me it was my problem to solve to get some windows in your home and it's taking over my mindset. So, I found out how to do it." I said "YAY! How do we do it?" He said he'd drive back up and talk to me about it.

He had to drive from Savannah, GA to Hoschton (a four-hour drive), but he did it and came all the way to tell me he couldn't eat or sleep. He was trying to figure out how to help me.

Then one day he told his boss about it. I said, "Why didn't you tell him sooner, before you went through this nightmare? He said, "I didn't believe anybody could get anything without hard cash or credit." So, he told me the boss said if they can put a lien on my property, they'd do it. I told the dude, "Lien all over it, winters coming, and my power bill is out of sight and we're freezing."

So, there you have it- God came through after standing in faith. It could happen. It did happen! This blew this guy's mind and he said it actually changed his life. He said he'd never forget me or this place. Okay, so here they come. Put the windows in, it was wonderful.

No plastic where raccoons or other species would be in the living room when you walked in, it was Heaven

The winter was super cold. It was the ice storm of the century that year. I remember it because the windows were so big and beautiful, looking out there, the ice hanging from the trees looked like a movie. We were coming along.

Jed was still pissed about everything no matter how we progressed, it was like he didn't want to do any of it, but couldn't get out of it. So, he'd stay focused on his race cars and buddies, and I'd figure out how to make the next move with our living arrangements.

Remember the heating and air guy? He helped me, but the temporary power pole was still an issue.

I was just waiting for the power company to come down on us at the time. I had made arrangements to pay the giant power bill off in payments. But, according to the guy, they were still coming back. Not knowing when or how something is going to happen always gives a kind of creepy feeling, kind of like waiting for the hammer to drop.

So, I was kind of scared since I didn't really know what they would do, or how you were supposed to do it right anyway. It was all a "super faith walk", which is the one reason I call this volume "Faith Walker". I found some doors at a yard sale and Coop put them in. Then I saved up for some French doors, which were so awesome.

I was jacked up, and then we got them put in, the windows and the doors – we were kickin! But the plank and the mote were still there. You still had to walk the plank to get in.

It was finally December, and it was freezing. I was worried about the power bills being so high and how was I going to ever get my temporary power pole problem taken care of.

It was Christmas day, there was a knock on the downstairs door early in the morning. I ran down to answer it, and there stood a man with a big smile on his face. He said, "I'm looking for Roxanne". I told him that was me, and he said his name was Lord. He said he wanted to tell me that for Christmas the power company decided to put me a real power pole in.

I couldn't believe that they wanted to do a good deed for someone for Christmas, so I jumped up and hugged his neck and said, "Thank God!" He said, "Yes, thank God." He went on to tell me that I was the talk of the power company and that they couldn't believe I had weathered the storm with the plastic on the windows and the whole deal and they all got together to give me a blessing.

I told Jed but he was never excited about anything. It was kind of a downer since I saw the Lord working. Basically, I said, "Winter, give it your best shot!" I was still living in the camper through all of this, and the kids were still in the basement.

They were ecstatic. You'd think after all that, I'd be ecstatic too, but I was over it. I felt like I had been pushed, prodded, tortured, and I was just downright over all of it.

I thought there was no way that normal people (whatever that is) would go through all that just to have a homestead.

6

Endurance Test

 I could drive down Highway 60 and see somebody building a house, and they'd be done, framed in, sheetrock, plants in the yard and living in their house in two months and what was I doing? Freezing, torturing myself, so I was basically mad. Mad at everything. I was living with a mean dude, walking the plank, having to wing everything I was doing, so I got mad at Jed one day and told him to "Bit me" and stormed out of the camper.

There was a big black dog he had, laying outside of the camper. I stormed out, lost my footing, stepped on the dog, and fell into the rocks. My arm popped out of socket. This was the icing on the cake. I was over it. I was slap fed up! Jed comes out to help me and I told him not to touch me!!!

I was throwing my own pity party. He backed off. I went in the camper and got on my bunk, in a lot of pain – I was crying out HELP ME! No money to go to hospital, a half-built house, two crummy trucks, and now I thought my arm was broke. Jed came in, got on the bunk beside me and said, "Let me see your arm."

I said "No way! Get away, get out of my life." This must be some kind of nightmare that I was surely waking up from. But no – he grabbed my arm, jerked it, and the thing popped back into the socket. It hurt so bad, but the relief was incredible.

When I saw the movie "Lethal Weapon" and his shoulder got disengaged, and he got up on that pole and popped it back in…

I could totally relate to that. One thing I know is you can't really be emotional when you were living that way, like I was.

No place for it- too hard on the daily for tears so I learned not to cry, and I think it was several years that I didn't cry. That's not good.

I wouldn't say I was callus; I was just over having to be the tough guy. No one else I knew was doing that. They all seemed to have it all wrapped up and I was on some ship out at sea by myself. The kids, Sammy and Dana would try to pull me out of it. They wanted to get a pool table.

So, I said, "Okay, we have to have something to do in the middle of nowhere. The pool table brought us common ground to group up and have fun. I happened to be a pool shark from Las Vegas cause when I was kid,I played pool for money and drugs to pay my bills – so I'd play the kids and their friends and Jed's friends.

47

The trucks were still working so it seemed like we were gaining some kind of ground, but like everyone else, we tried to look at what we didn't have instead of what we did. The half glass empty mentality. Jed kept telling me to not give up and "Keep on Truckin" but trying to get a loan to complete the house, sheetrock and carpet – I was just over it.

I had one of the first fax machines on the planet, so I'd fax loan officers my plan and wait for a response and because my situation was so weird, no one would help me. I was getting discouraged, gaining weight, feeling sluggish, just plain over it. I hope you know that God himself knows how much you can take.

Then one day, out of the blue – I got a fax. Remember the lady in the Cadillac that brought me down to the slab, and sold me the dirt? Well, here she comes again! I couldn't believe it; she had a deal for me to finish the house. The deal was crazy!

The stipulations were so unreasonable I couldn't believe it – but then I could. Here they were: They would loan me the forty thousand to finish the house, I had to have everything done in thirty days including concrete, yard, all of it or they'd take twenty percent. Now it was dead of winter – January in the North Georgia Mountains. I was beside myself. Take the deal??? Finish and be done with it in thirty days???

7

Deal Accepted

Well, I took the deal. Now, the deal was a hell of a deal, okay. It really was. So, immediately I had thirty days to figure out how I was going to find sheet rockers, people to pour concrete and workers to just completely finish the house, meaning the yard had to be manicured. I mean the whole deal. The whole nine.

So, I had to get a little outline going. Ya know, I haven't really done it before, but it's just something you do. You put your mind to it and start writing it down on paper and then the vision will come to pass.

So, that's what I did – I wrote it all down. I figured out who I needed, what I needed, and how much I needed, including time. Then I started hunting the people to make it happen in 30 days. So, it got pretty interesting, to say the least.

Remember, we're right in the middle of January in the Georgia mountains. It was freezing and I didn't know anything about concrete, but I figured out really quick that you can't pour concrete in 32 degree weather. The guy said, "Look lady, you can't order concrete right now – its freezing outside."

The crew I dug up was a bunch of dudes who were very cool. They were ready to do a massive concrete pour in that red mud and get that plank straightened out so we could actually walk around the property. Well, the leader of the pack agreed and told me the same thing the concrete company told me: "It couldn't be done", "it was too cold".

ROCK

I said, "Dude, I have this saying: "If there's a will, there's a way." You have 7 or 8 guys who all gotta get paid. If you just think on it, there's gotta be a way. What's the way? He walked away for a minute then he said "Okay, we build fires." So, I said, "Cut down the trees out there if you need to." So we started fires…

I figured my budget on concrete was some small amount like 5 grand or something and you had to order it by yards. The concrete guy was right down the road from me down highway 60, so I started ordering it. Well, when I drew it out how I wanted it to look.

There was a lot of concrete required. Remember, it had to be a specific temperature before they could pour it.

So here comes the concrete trucks. The guys have fires built everywhere and they're ready to pour. They come up to the camper and they grab their check and the rest of them kept coming.

These guys were working so hard, bless their hearts. They were doing a really great job! As I started to see it take form, I knew I needed more concrete, so I kept ordering more and more.

I had probably 15 trucks outside. Well, we didn't have a gate, so they parked outside the perimeter. These guys were ready to pour, and they did it!

8

Concrete Lesson

 If you saw it today, you'd think WOW! You really would. So, I go through the concrete thing and the men were just amazed at the tenacity to pour!

Anyways, Jed was freaked out the whole time. He didn't know what I was doing. He was out there while I had the sheet rockers in the house.

They couldn't come when the concrete guys were there; there was a process to it, and since there was a process to it and I had no clue what that process was. I was basically giving it my all to see what I thought it should look like.

Well, you know what it's like when you're doing something you've never done before…..

so I was counting on Old Man Coop. He

couldn't believe it! He was the cabinet maker, so he was in the house working on the cabinets. Remember, I said it had to be a done deal, so Old Man Coop was absolutely awesome.

He helped me in so many ways just keeping me pumped up in general. Well, in the process, he helped me keep moving, basically.

Another thing with the concrete guys; it wasn't your average concrete job and my budget wasn't cutting it, so I basically stuck my neck out in faith. But this was before I even knew what FAITH was; but I stuck my neck out there anyways, and made a deal with the leader of the pack of the concrete guys.

ROCK

I told them I'd cut a check every week until I got them taken care of. They did a really good job. They really did. So that part was done.

Once the concrete was secure, everyone could walk on it, drive on it, basically do anything on it. This really made finishing a lot easier because we could get in and out of the house without walking the plank. Walking the plank was quite the feat!

9

Party and Stress

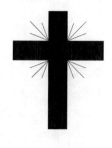
So we had a small party, ya know, busted out a bottle of tequila, and we got drunk. Everybody was stressed out, I could hardly blame them, right!

We were doing something that most people wouldn't even attempt to do but these guys were really good at it. So now here come the sheet rockers. I didn't know how sheetrock went. I didn't know anything about the process.

What I did know was that the guy that was going to inspect in 30 days. So, the first thing I pictured was the concrete, so since it was down. The next thing was the sheet rock and so on and so forth. Well, here they all go, they're kicking. So, I'm down to, I don't know, say fifteen days in, and I find out that the inspector was going to inspect on a specific day; January 31st.

Remember, if it wasn't completed by the deadline, they would take 20% of the money. Well, remember my buddy at the pawn shop, my broker Phil? He had my back, he really did. He said, "Just do it Rock, I'll help you out… If you can't pay these boys or something, just bring me a check and I'll hold it for you until however long it took."

So, Jed had this great idea. He had this who was a mason down in Live Oak, Florida, which is exactly where I was taken to right out of Vegas.

But this dude was the king of mason. He came up to do our fireplaces and other stuff that needed to be finished in the house. So here these guys come, I'm still in the camper. I got my little bunk and table (little office basically). The dudes walk in and one of them says, "Hey listen, we're gonna start getting to work in the house but I need to ask you something. Do you know how to roll?" I said, "What do you mean?", and he replied, "Do you know how to roll pot, like weed"? I said, "Yeah, I mean I ain't rolled any in a minute, but I'm actually pretty good at it."

So, he hands me a baggie, a GALLON SIZE BAGGIE of weed. He said, "Can you roll us up about 10 joints cause we gotta get started here." I'm like "10 JOINTS?! Sure buddy, whatever you gotta do." So, I sat down, rolled them up and they got in there, did what they needed to do.

I waited a while to check out their work, but next thing you know, here comes the guys to the camper saying, "Hey Rock, can you roll us some more?" It had only been a couple hours!

He said, "Well, we already smoked it all man," so I said, "So are y'all some serious pot smokers?" and he goes "Yeah, I mean if you want us to get the job done right that's what we gotta have." So, I took care of them, but I told them I'd be back to check in on the job

I couldn't believe it. I thought to myself, this guy does really good work! He's a master at what he does. He was free handing this fireplace with these rocks that was just absolutely amazing.

He says to me, "Pick the rocks you like so I can put them where you want them."

There was a fireplace upstairs and downstairs have different type of rocks: downstairs was slate, upstairs was stone. This guy was an absolute master at what he did. He was so impressive, it really blew my mind. I told him, "Dude, you are an absolute master at this!

You are! This is your trade! I didn't know you were THIS GOOD!" But there's a little something else these guys did during their two weeks working on the house.

10

Bunked in the Basement

 There were mattresses in the basement mainly for the kids, but the crew slept on them during the day while the kids were at school. Remember, the kids are teenagers at this point. One day, I come downstairs to look at the crew's work. It's around 4pm in the afternoon and these guys are standing in a circle and MY KIDS are INSIDE this circle. I look at my kids and they're passing the weed to my kids.

I yelled "Y'all get out of this circle, you ain't smoking weed with these guys!" I started yelling at the leader, I said, "Dude, you don't come here and start getting my kids to smoke pot with you. You are here to do a job.

you wanna do your own thing, that's a different story, that's your thing, but don't come in here trying to infect my kids! You better talk to me first because I can be kind of a "bitty". (That's a nice word for "B I T C H") I just flat told em, don't do it again!

So, the kids were punished and put on restriction. The masonry dudes are doing their thing and the kids are in trouble. They were probably a couple days out from finishing, so I was asking them to do tile work in the bathroom that I had seen in a magazine. They was so good so I'm glad they could actually do it!

I could tell they were about ready to leave and I was trying to make sure they had everything done and he was like, "We're running out of weed, we gotta get out of here". I was like, "Come on, really, I'm paying you to do a job." He said he had to go at a certain time, "Sorry about your luck," so I said, "Okay dude."

11

Brand New Crew

 In the meantime, I didn't know you had your sheet rockers and your mud tapers. I didn't know they all went together. All I knew at this point was it needed to get done.

We had cathedral ceilings which were super high and the crew kept telling me all about the challenge and I acted like I knew what was happening.

Honestly, I really didn't have a clue what was next. However, I looked mean and I looked like I knew what i was doing.

The crew asked me when they were all done with their jobs, "Where do we go next?" They thought I was the contractor! I said, "No, I'm a trucker!" They were shocked! I said, "Yeah, I'm a trucker! We're just doing this because we need somewhere to live." They said, "What?! Well, you're really good at it. You just tell us where to go next and we'll go."

I laughed and thought well, it was kind of the same thing dispatching trucks and dispatching these men to the job sites. Since I was always the leader of the men, I would basically bark out: "Go here, go there".

That's just who I was, that's actually who I AM! By the grace of God, in the meantime, these guys were mortified because I couldn't tell them where to go next. I'm down to the wire, I have a week out. Well, the cabinets weren't finished, and Coop was 70 years old, so I wasn't going to try to push him.

ROCK

The carpet wasn't in yet, and there was a lot of stuff still not done at this point. It's been my experience in life that people like the way stuff looks like on the outside even if they don't necessarily know what's going on in the inside, but if it looks good on the outside, they'll usually buy it.

12

Stick Dog

So, that's the way I went with it. We concentrated on the outside of the place and make sure it looked good, this meant the yard, painting, whatever had to happen on the outside, so it looked like a finished product.

Needless to say, it was so stressful that I couldn't take much more. I was probably about four to six days out and the landscapers that were doing the yard had it looking really good outside. Remember the black lab I tripped over?

He was a stick dog named Buddy.

If you threw a stick, he would run and fetch it, and he'd sit at your feet and pant, pant, pant until you threw it again. He was pretty fast. He'd be back and forth, back and forth, throw the stick, fetch the stick.

Old Man Coop tells me, "Look, I don't think I'm going to get done with these cabinets. I'm trying." Basically, the majority of it looked good. There was just a lot that needed to be done upstairs. We made sure the basement and the exterior looked really good.

Only five days out, everyone's freaking…we're out of money; the whole nine. It's time, here comes the big day.Here's where the stick dog comes in. The inspector for the mortgage company shows up. He pulls up downstairs so I'm thanking God that he went to the basement first because that's the ONLY PART at this point that's even fully finished.

ROCK

Well, he gets out of the car and he's a 70 year old man with a cane. I look over at him and walk down to meet him. I shake his hand, he tells me his name, I tell him my name, etc. He says, "Ready for your inspection?" I say, "Oh yeah, I'm ready."

He said the yard looked really good, so I thanked him. Then comes the dog...so the stick dog puts a stick down at the inspector's feet and he starts throwing the stick for the dog. So back and forth, here comes the dog and the stick. The man says, "You know, I really like this dog. He is a very cool dog!" I said, "Well, if he's bothering you, I'll get rid of him."

He takes his cane and starts walking towards the door. The whole way in, I'm praying please have mercy – don't go upstairs. The cabinets weren't done, a bunch of stuff upstairs wasn't completed.

He walks over and says the yard looks great, mentions the concrete is down, all the time stick dog is still at his feet...

At this point he peaks in the double French doors downstairs and checks out the basement and says, "Well it looks really good to me". He asks if everything upstairs was finished, and I lie like a dog..." I say, "Yeah." He says, "I guess it's your lucky day, you passed inspection, and you have a really cool dog too."

I reply, "Well, thank you sir, I really appreciate it." I was not trying to look too excited and jump around and look like a lunatic, I said, "Thank you sir". He said, "Well, I guess my job's done here. I'll report in that you finished the job and you can carry on."

"I appreciate you sir." I can't tell you how relieved I was about the stick dog. He petted the dog like 12 times before he even got in the car. I honestly believe that God will put things in the way for you to help you out in different ways.

Obviously this was a very stressful 30 days. All the men were stressed. Anybody and everybody involved were stressed out. So, it goes without saying, when we finally go the OKAY, it was so awesome! As we continue in the next volume, I will show you again how awesome it is when we walk by Faith.

Peace be with you and KEEP ON TRUCKIN!

I hope the eyes of understanding will be enlightened as you read the Volumes of the Farm to Table Series. I hope as you read the next 16 volumes, you all see that God is leading you to a place you can't afford and to a fight YOU can't win alone. Whatever adversity you go through, HOLD FAST – HE WILL bring you through!

Author's Note

As I write the different stories of how I overcame the obstacles that have come into my life, if you notice, in the Volume III of Farm to Table, each and every enemy came to stop the building project of The Ponderosa, which is now a giant ministry operating full-time under the hand of God, in the prisons, in the streets, and on the land, that I'm telling you about (The Ponderosa).

I declare and decree over you right now that you will increase!

Isaiah 51:2 "May the Lord bless you and increase you more and more"

Psalm 71 says "I declare and decree He will increase your greatness and comfort you on every side"

Acts 9:22 "He will increase your strength to confound your adversaries"

Proverbs 9:11 "the most High God will increase the years of your life"

You will increase day by day, the most high God, in the name of Jesus, will give you joy and prosperity and will give you strength to finish reading all volumes of The Farm to Table Series and prosper you as you read.

"Godspeed"

What does "GODSPEED" mean?
An expression of Good Wishes to a person starting a journey. Otherwise saying, "May God grant success to you!"

What does "Shalom" mean?
It means nothing missing - wholeness for everything and all things.
When someone says this to you, they are wishing you peace.

Territory is important. This series was birthed in Northeast Georgia mountains of Toccoa, Georgia.

As we walk this journey together, you'll see in my story just how many times a "higher power" has intervened for me. I really want you to know who this higher power truly is—His name is Jesus Christ. During my story, I called Him "God" a lot. Truthfully, it was indeed God. For the time I was living through what you just read, I really didn't understand who Jesus was ... and is. But I do now.

Maybe you don't know Jesus either, and that's okay. I'd like to suggest that you look at your own journey. Have there been things you just couldn't explain? Since there isn't any such thing as a coincidence, then who was it exactly that intervened in your life?

I encourage you to take a moment and think about it.

If you want peace, love, joy, and faith, all you have to do is start with a sincere prayer, an example of which follows ...

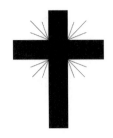

Jesus,

I confess that I have sinned and fallen short of your glory.

I believe that you suffered and died on the cross for me,

And when you did that,

You paid the full price for the punishment due me, for my sins.

Please forgive me for my sins,

And accept me into your kingdom.

Until right now,

I have only lived for myself.

From now on,

I will only live for you.

Thank you for your incredible sacrifice,

And please also show me

How to help others.

When it is my time,

I look forward to being received

Into your glorious presence.

Please come into my life

Now,

And forever …

Welcome to the family!

Don't stop now, there's work to be done.

For more info on this book, go to www.amazon.com

Notes

Notes

_____

_____

_____

_____

_____

_____

_____

Notes

Made in the USA
Columbia, SC
17 June 2024

36765672R00050